ESSENTIAL

GOOD

CW00346454

COMPUTER
TROUBLESHOOTING

ABOUT THIS BOOK

Computer Troubleshooting is an easy-to-follow guide to the
Windows Me suite of products available for troubleshooting a
PC, and assumes little or no prior knowledge of the subject.

THE PERSONAL COMPUTER HAS changed our lives in so many ways, allowing us to look after our home finances, produce highly designed documents, and spend hours surfing the internet. But most users assume that a PC can manage its own affairs despite our bad habits, poor practices, and sometimes thoughtless use of these highly technical and complex machines. The aim of this book is to help you optimize some performance aspects of your PC and to avoid common problems. You will discover how to maintain your hard drive, keep it clean by defragmenting the files, check for viruses, and delete old files that clutter up and slow down your PC, as well as finding out how to prepare for any emergency that may arise.

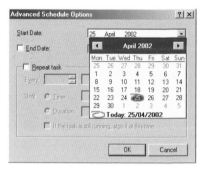

The chapters and the subsections in the book use a step-by-step approach that takes you methodically through each procedure. Almost every step is illustrated by screen shots to show what you should be looking at during the procedures.

The book contains several other features that make it easier to absorb the quantity of information provided. Cross-references are shown within the text as left- or right-hand page icons: ⬁ and ⬀. The page number within the icon and the reference are shown at the foot of the page.

As well as the step-by-step sections, there are boxes that explain the meaning of unfamiliar terms and abbreviations, and give additional information to take your knowledge beyond that provided on the rest of the page. Finally, at the back, you will find a glossary explaining new terms and a comprehensive index.

ESSENTIAL **DK** COMPUTERS

GOOD PRACTICE

COMPUTER TROUBLESHOOTING

ANDREW EASTON

LONDON, NEW YORK, MUNICH, MELBOURNE, DELHI

EDITOR Richard Gilbert
SENIOR ART EDITOR Sarah Cowley
DTP DESIGNER Rajen Shah
PRODUCTION CONTROLLER Sarah Sherlock

MANAGING EDITOR Adèle Hayward
MANAGING ART EDITOR Marianne Markham
CATEGORY PUBLISHER Stephanie Jackson

Produced for Dorling Kindersley Limited by
Design Revolution Limited, Queens Park Villa,
30 West Drive, Brighton, East Sussex BN2 0QW
EDITORIAL DIRECTOR Ian Whitelaw
SENIOR DESIGNER Andy Ashdown
PROJECT EDITOR John Watson
DESIGNER Andrew Easton

First published in Great Britain in 2000 by
Dorling Kindersley Limited,
80 Strand, London WC2R 0RL

Revised edition 2002

A Penguin Company

2 4 6 8 10 9 7 5 3 1

A CIP catalogue record for this book is available from the British Library.

ISBN 0-7513-6431-2

Colour reproduced by Colourscan, Singapore
Printed and bound in Italy by Graphicom

For our complete catalogue visit
www.dk.com

CONTENTS

ABOUT YOUR PC

In a competition for causing heartache, frustration, and sometimes physical violence, the PC would be in the running for first prize; but it doesn't have to be this way.

LOOKING AFTER YOUR PC

Most of us don't realize (or ignore) how much we abuse the machines we depend on. However, with a little knowledge and a small amount of time, the sometimes tense relationship you have with your computer can be made easier.

RECURRING TASKS

Most computer users follow an endless round of activities including installing and uninstalling software, downloading a new version, moving files, making a copy, deleting the old version, and inevitably forgetting where a particular file is saved.

Every computer is subject to these events and, over time, they may result in bad files, duplicate files, unused files, and any amount of unnecessary data clogging up, and slowing down, the performance levels of your machine.

Although the PC is built to cope with an astonishing amount of data, there comes a time when you need to assess exactly what you do and don't need, and carry out a major cleanup of your system. This book introduces a number of simple methods to tidy up your computer.

Although a crash-free computer can't be guaranteed 100%, you can help to reduce the possibility of future problems occurring.

MAKING A STARTUP DISK!

Later in this book there is a section explaining how to protect yourself if your computer will not start up 🗋. A startup disk takes only moments to create and will prove to be an invaluable asset when the time comes to use it.

Startup Disk
January

Your computer has to deal with a colossal amount of data and keep track of its movements.

HELP IS AT HAND

For a PC to operate correctly, there are hundreds of components, as well as the software, that must all work together. Inevitably, performance problems do occur as a result of glitches, and these may either be trivial or, rarely, terminal. The actions you take to resolve a problem when one occurs may have an effect, but sometimes they are inappropriate. For example, restarting your computer can clear a fault, but if your machine is running slowly, restarting your PC is unlikely to solve the problem. Part of the answer lies in knowing what is available

to help you. Among the software on your computer, there are tools for preventive maintenance to help stop faults from developing, and others to rectify problems when they do occur. For example, later in this section we will show you how to clean your PC's hard drives of unwanted files. We will then delve deeper and explain how to use utilities such as ScanDisk and Disk Defragmenter to examine, clean up, and repair broken and damaged files on the hard drive. These are simple, but effective, procedures and techniques to keep your PC in working order.

THE WORKING PC

If you are new to computers, you may be uncertain about the meanings of the terms that are used to describe the different elements that make a PC work. Here we explain the differences between peripherals, software, and hardware.

Peripherals
A peripheral is a piece of equipment that is used for either input (such as a keyboard or scanner) or output (such as a printer, monitor, or external modem) and can be connected to your computer. Most peripherals require a piece of software to make them run. This is known as a driver and is supplied along with the peripheral. Upgrades to the drivers can sometimes be downloaded from the internet.

Software
Software comes in many shapes and sizes and is usually supplied on a CD-ROM, unless of course you are downloading it from the internet ●

Hardware
Computer hardware consists of all the physical elements of the system, including the main PC unit, monitor, keyboard, mouse, and any additional peripherals.

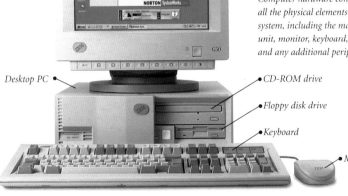

Monitor ●

Desktop PC ●

● *CD-ROM drive*

● *Floppy disk drive*

● *Keyboard*

● *Mouse*

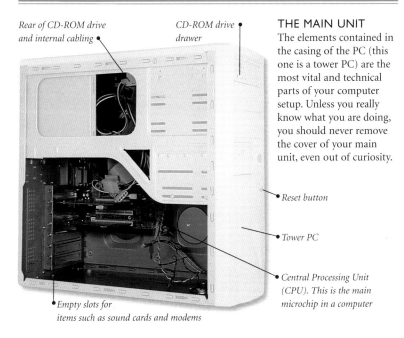

Rear of CD-ROM drive and internal cabling

CD-ROM drive drawer

CD-ROM drive

Empty slots for items such as sound cards and modems

• *Reset button*

• *Tower PC*

• *Central Processing Unit (CPU). This is the main microchip in a computer*

THE MAIN UNIT

The elements contained in the casing of the PC (this one is a tower PC) are the most vital and technical parts of your computer setup. Unless you really know what you are doing, you should never remove the cover of your main unit, even out of curiosity.

HARDWARE

Hardware is made up of the parts of your computer that you can see and touch. The keyboard, mouse, scanner, printer, modem, and monitor are all hardware, as is the PC system box, which may be either a tower unit or a desktop unit. The PC system box houses the microchips, the related circuitry that make the input and output peripherals work, as well as the drives, including the hard disk drive, which store all your software. It is also the component to which all the peripherals are connected. The PC is adaptable and can be easily upgraded.

SOFTWARE

Your computer needs software, or programs, for the hardware to function, and for you to do anything useful with your computer. Software comes in many forms – from simple utilities to immense computer games. Most software is now supplied on CD-ROM.

Computers have more speed and capacity than ten years ago and software developers make the most of these developments by pushing the hardware faster and harder. Programs have outgrown floppy disks as a means of storing them, and now software is supplied on higher capacity CD-ROMs.

BASIC TROUBLESHOOTING

In this chapter, we will deal with fast recovery from problems, isolating and identifying problems, closing a crashed program, and removing unnecessary software and dead shortcuts.

BASIC RECOVERY STEPS

When troubleshooting, remember that computers are completely logical and that there is always a rational reason why a problem has occurred. Correctly identifying the reason and finding a solution will be easier if you work step-by-step. However, try one or more of these basic recovery steps first when you next become aware that your computer is beginning to malfunction.

QUIT AND RESTART

● Quit the program and restart the computer to reload the operating software. Minor problems, especially temporary memory problems, can be solved in this way.

SAVE AS AND REOPEN

● Save your work under a different name and location by using the **Save As** option, quit the program, restart it, and open the new version of your work.

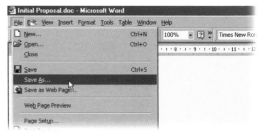

REINSTALLING

● If your software has become corrupted, reinstalling it from the original disks may often resolve the problem.

*The Microsoft Office install options include a **Repair Office** function*

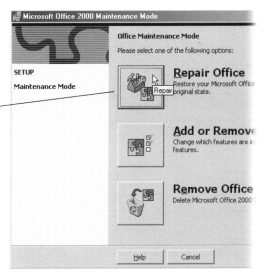

DISK REPAIR UTILITY

● Use a disk repair utility, such as Norton Utilities, that scans and repairs your hard drive and carries out other system maintenance.

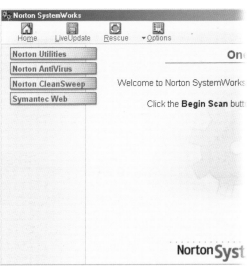

ISOLATING A PROBLEM

The preceding steps should help you to recover from an emergency, but to find out what went wrong, you may need to move on to problem isolation. A distinction to draw is between hardware and software problems. Most systems consist of only a few major components: monitor, printer, hard drive, CD-ROM drive, and the system box, and each can be isolated to identify a problem. As far as software is concerned, every computer is different, but they can share characteristic problems, the cause of which can be identified by isolating suspect applications.

HARDWARE ISOLATION

● A simple example is that if you have no display on the monitor, check the power lights on both the computer and the monitor. If the computer light is on but the monitor light is off, check the monitor for burning smells, have a look at all the cables, particularly the power cords, and listen for a high-pitched whine or squealing sound. All of these (apart from the cables) are symptoms of a failed monitor.

Do not open the monitor
Never take the back off a monitor. Opening the casing of a monitor exposes you to dangerously high voltages from 10,000 to 50,000 volts, even when the monitor is disconnected. You are endangering your personal safety by attempting to repair a monitor. Limit activities to identifying the symptoms before seeking professional help.

SWAPPING COMPONENTS

If your hardware problem has symptoms that are less obvious, it may be possible to isolate the problem by swapping a peripheral with another model of the same type. If the problem continues with a replacement peripheral, try swapping the cables. If that cures the problem, you have isolated the cause to a fault in the original cable. If not, the problem lies with the system box, which will probably need professional attention.

If you have no display, and yet the computer is switched on and running, the monitor or its power supply has failed.

WINDOWS ME HELP SYSTEM

There are times when even the most proficient PC user will bump into a problem that cannot be easily answered without a little assistance. Microsoft **Help and Support** is an invaluable resource for solving the most basic of "how to" scenarios, to complex networking problems. Chances are that if you have a problem, you will find a solution here. There are also some useful troubleshooting guides and even links to the internet for on-line assistance.

OPEN HELP AND SUPPORT

● To open the main **Help and Support** window, click on the **Start** button and then on **Help**.

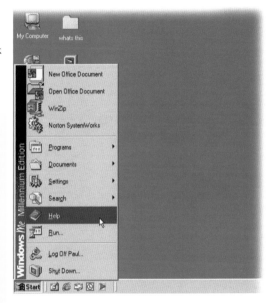

At Startup..
When your PC first starts up, it puts itself through a checking process, making sure that everything is working correctly and determining which hardware devices are installed. It also works out whether you are booting the PC from its own hard disk, or a CD-ROM (if you were having problems, you may want to boot from the Windows Me CD-ROM – see the section on using a startup disk ⌐).

| 58 | **About Startup Disks** |

● The main Microsoft **Help and Support** window opens. This introductory page offers you a guide to basic computing with Windows Me, including how to use the internet, printing, scanning, and playing games.

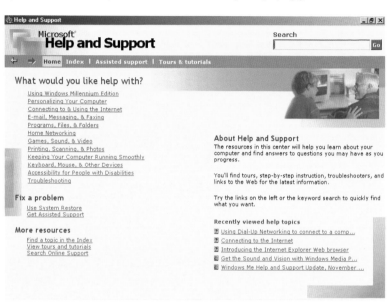

● To get the necessary help, click on the appropriate hyperlinked text.

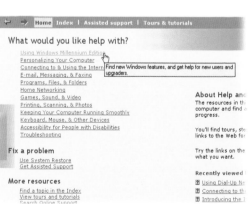

What is a hyperlink?
A hyperlink can be an image, table, or text that links to another item once it is clicked on.

● Near the top of the window, you will find an index that links to all the items contained within **Help and Support**. You can also click on **Assisted support**, which has its own links to the internet, or **Tours & tutorials**.

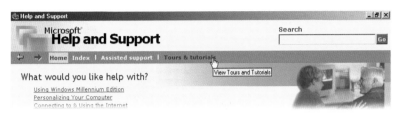

● At the top right of the window, you will find a **Search** panel. Type in a key word to discover more about a particular topic.

● For this example, type in the word **clock** and then click on the **Go** button.
● The results of the search are displayed on the right-hand side of the window.

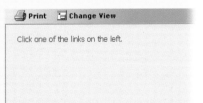

You searched for *clock*

Help & Information:

🔲 Changing the elapsed time before hard disk turns off
🔲 Changing the elapsed time before computer goes on standby or hibernate
🔲 Changing your computer's time
🔲 Changing your computer's time zone
🔲 Changing the way your computer displays the time

🖨 Print   📄 Change View

Click one of the links on the left.

● In this example, we have clicked on the link that says **Changing your computer's time**. You will see that Windows Me's instructions on how to do this appears in the right-hand side of the window.

● The topic is displayed on the right-hand side of the window.

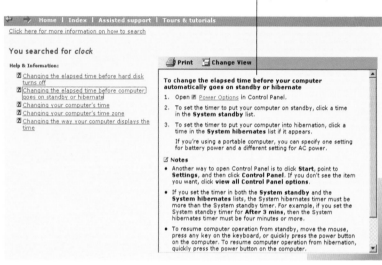

● The search result can be either printed by clicking on the **Print** button, or viewed in its own window by clicking on the **Change View** button.

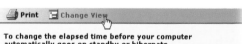

To change the screen back to how it looked originally, click on the Change View button again

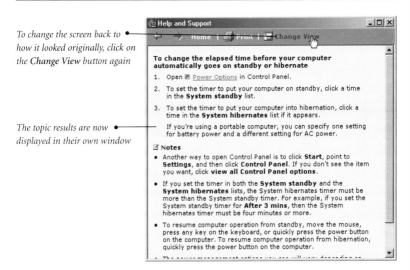

To change the elapsed time before your computer automatically goes on standby or hibernate

1. Open 🖼 Power Options in Control Panel.

2. To set the timer to put your computer on standby, click a time in the **System standby** list.

3. To set the timer to put your computer into hibernation, click a time in the **System hibernates** list if it appears.

   If you're using a portable computer, you can specify one setting for battery power and a different setting for AC power.

The topic results are now displayed in their own window

🗹 **Notes**

- Another way to open Control Panel is to click **Start**, point to **Settings**, and then click **Control Panel**. If you don't see the item you want, click **view all Control Panel options**.

- If you set the timer in both the **System standby** and the **System hibernates** lists, the System hibernates timer must be more than the System standby timer. For example, if you set the System standby timer for **After 3 mins**, then the System hibernates timer must be four minutes or more.

- To resume computer operation from standby, move the mouse, press any key on the keyboard, or quickly press the power button on the computer. To resume computer operation from hibernation, quickly press the power button on the computer.

● If you find that you have delved rather deeply into the help system, simply click on the **Home** button.

TROUBLESHOOTING WEBSITES

http://www.troubleshooters.com
This site is a great starting point for any troubleshooting or debugging task.

http://wombat.doc.ic.ac.uk
This site is a free online dictionary of computing.

www.fhsu.edu/cis/es/howto.html
Links to a number of troubleshooting and technical queries sites.

http://zdnet.com/sr/columns/glass
A site that welcomes technical queries by email.

www.techadvice.com/tech/C/
ComputerTS.htm
A site with preprepared questions and answers in text format, with a number of links to other web pages and websites to refer to if you can't find what you're looking for here.

CLOSING A CRASHED PROGRAM

Making a diagnosis of why your computer is not functioning correctly is not always an easy task, and there are numerous reasons why your machine may have failed. Faults sometimes rectify themselves without an obvious reason, but from time to time your computer will need some help to free itself from a problem.

WHEN YOUR PC FREEZES

One of the most common problems to occur with a PC is when everything "freezes" or "locks up" while you are using an application, and the mouse and keyboard will not respond. This is rarely the fault of the hardware – the problem usually lies with the software in use.

1 FREEZES AND LOCKUPS

● First, give your PC a moment to sort itself out. Never hastily turn the PC off as this can lead to further problems.

2 USING CONTROL, ALT, AND DELETE

● After waiting a while, try to close the locked-up application by using the key combination of:
Ctrl + Alt + Del.
● Holding down these keys simultaneously should display the **Close Program** dialog box.

3 CLOSE PROGRAM DIALOG BOX

● This box shows all the applications that are currently running on your system, and next to the locked-up application there should be a message that reads: **Not Responding**.

● Click on the name of the application in the dialog box, and click on the **End Task** button.

4 END TASK OR SHUTDOWN

● If the software still refuses to close immediately, wait a few moments before pressing [Ctrl] + [Alt] + [Del] again, which should reboot your machine. If the computer still won't respond, then you will have to press the reset button on the front of your PC, if you have one. If you don't have a reset button, then you will need to turn the machine off, wait for 15 seconds, and then turn it on again in the conventional way.

Off button ●

Reset button ●

REMOVING UNNECESSARY FILES

The performance of your PC can be slowed down by the accumulation of unnecessary files. Deleting files one at a time can be a lengthy business. Here, we explain how to locate a folder containing these files and how to delete them.

1 SELECT WINDOWS EXPLORER

● The files that are to be deleted are temporary files stored in a folder called **Temp** within the **Windows** folder. These files are left in the **Temp** folder when your computer crashes, and can safely be deleted.

● To find them, begin by clicking on the **Start** button, select **Programs**, and then **Windows Explorer**.

2 FINDING TEMPORARY FILES

● Click on the plus (+) sign next to **My Computer**, then **Local Disk** and finally the **Windows** folder, scroll down to the **Temp** folder and click on it.

● Its contents are displayed in the right-hand panel.

The **Temp** *folder is contained within the* **Windows** *folder* ●

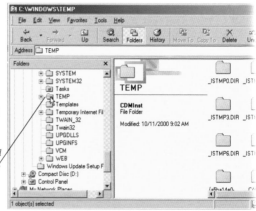

3 SORTING FILES BY TYPE

● Firstly, click on the **View** drop-down-menu and select **Details** from the list.
● Next, scroll along the window and click on the **Type** column header to list the files by type, then scroll down to see the start of the **TMP** files.

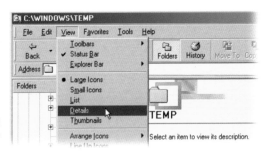

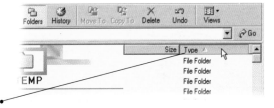

The Type column header ●

4 SELECTING THE TMP FILES

● Click on the first **TMP** file, scroll down to display the last **TMP** file and, while holding down the Shift key, click on the last **TMP** file to select them all.

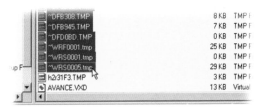

5 SELECTING THE DELETE OPTION

● Click on **File** in the menu bar and select **Delete**.
● An alert box asks you to confirm that the files are to be deleted. Click on **Yes**, and the files are deleted.

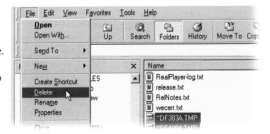

CLEANING UTILITIES

Many problems can be prevented by keeping your hard disk well organized. Windows provides three tools for this task, and commercial cleanup software is also readily available.

USING SCANDISK

ScanDisk can check for damaged files and make sure that your hard disk is correctly storing information. It can also be set up to correct any problems automatically. ScanDisk also looks for files and folders that have invalid file names, dates, and times, and corrects these problems more thoroughly and quickly than is possible by using manual methods.

First aid for files
ScanDisk checks for damage and carries out repairs.

1 OPENING SCANDISK
● Click on the **Start** button, then select: **Programs, Accessories, System Tools**, and finally ScanDisk.

2 THOROUGH OR STANDARD?

● When the **ScanDisk** dialog box opens, select the hard drive, **Local Disk** (C:), as the drive to be scanned.
● As this may be a first-time scan, click on the **Thorough** radio button to select that type of scan.
● Click in the **Automatically fix errors** check box.

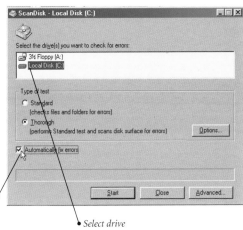

Automatically fix errors check box

Select drive

3 OTHER CHOICES

● Once you have selected the **Thorough** test, the **Options** button becomes available. Clicking on this button opens the **Surface Scan Options** dialog box, which provides scanning options. The standard test, which scans the system and data areas, is performed by default. ScanDisk can then look for any physical damage to your computer. You can also choose which specific areas of your disk are to be scanned. Click on **OK** to return to the main ScanDisk window.

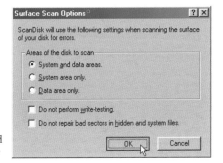

ADVANCED OPTIONS

By clicking on the **Advanced** button in the **Scandisk** dialog box, you can access options that include tests to deal with lost file fragments and invalid files. There is also the opportunity to create a log file so that you can see what has been fixed and what file problems have been found.

4 BEGINNING THE SCAN

● Once you are satisfied with your selections, begin the scan by clicking on the **Start** button in the **ScanDisk** dialog.

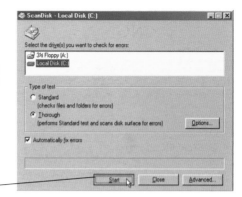

Click on Start

● ScanDisk runs through its scanning operation, checking disks and folders, as well as the physical surface of the hard drive. The **Checking folders** bar at the foot of the dialog box provides feedback on the program's progress.

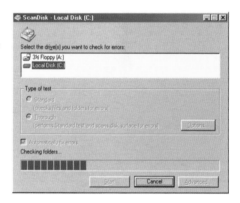

5 THE SCANDISK RESULTS

● The scanning and fixing of your disk will take some time. If you have chosen to scan one disk at a time, click **Close** when the first one has finished, and you can then choose the next disk to be scanned.

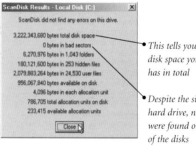

● *This tells you how much disk space your machine has in total*

● *Despite the size of this hard drive, no bad sectors were found on the surface of the disks*

USING DISK CLEANUP

Windows also contains a piece of software called Disk Cleanup. This program offers options to select files to search for and possibly delete, which creates more free disk space. This is a safe method if you are uncertain about deleting files.

1 OPENING DISK CLEANUP
● Click on the **Start** button, then select **Programs, Accessories, System Tools,** and finally **Disk Cleanup**.

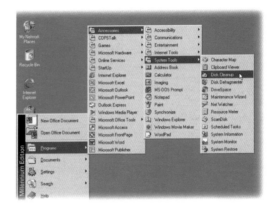

2 SELECTING THE DRIVE
● Disk Cleanup asks you which drive you would like to clean. With the majority of computers the hard drive is (**C:**), and this is the drive to be cleaned.

3 FREE SPACE
● Disk Cleanup then calculates how much free space it can create for you.

4 DESCRIPTION DIALOG

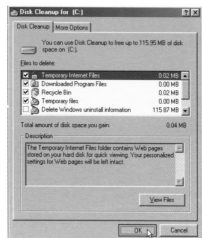

● In the next dialog box, Disk Cleanup tells you exactly how much space it can free up by deleting unnecessary files, such as temporary internet files, offline web pages, downloaded program files, the Recycle Bin (this means emptying files from the bin, not deleting it!), and other temporary files.

● Select the file types that you want Disk Cleanup to delete by clicking once in each of the check boxes next to them. It is best to accept each of Disk Cleanup's recommended file types.

● Once you have selected the items that you want to clean up, click on OK.

CLEANUP ROUTINES

If you are a fairly frequent user, you could establish a weekly cleaning schedule. Once you have carried out the first thorough clean as described in this section, the process can be quickly carried out.

5 BEGINNING THE CLEANUP

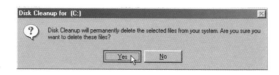

● As a final step before starting, a confirmation panel opens. Click on Yes.

6 FINISHING THE CLEANUP

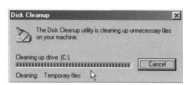

● After working through the selected options, Disk Cleanup shuts down automatically and you are returned to the Desktop.

USING DISK DEFRAGMENTER

Through normal use, files on a hard disk are broken up and scattered instead of being placed together. This is known as fragmentation and means that the computer has to work harder to gather all the information it needs to perform the required tasks. Disk Defragmenter reconstructs the fragmented files, meaning that they will load faster as the computer does not have to spend time looking for them. Disk Defragmenter also reorganizes files by putting those that are most frequently used at the start of your hard drive to speed up the working process.

HOW DOES FRAGMENTATION HAPPEN?

Fragmentation is not something that you can physically see or be aware of at the time it occurs. The two panels below illustrate how fragmentation occurs. The process has been simplified to provide a basic representation, although in reality disk fragmentation is very complex and depends on a large number of variables.

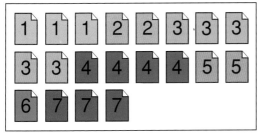

Your hard disk – week one.

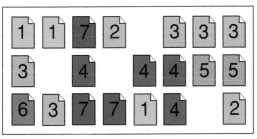

Your hard disk – week three; the files have started to be fragmented.

THE FRAGMENTATION PROCESS

In week one, the files show no fragmentation. However, by week three, there is evidence of fragmentation. This may be due to old software being uninstalled, work being carried out on existing documents, or scanning and saving new images. If a file is opened, added to, and saved, the enlarged file may be split up and placed wherever there is room. After a while, the file structure becomes severely fractured. Defragmenting not only cleans up the drive, it can also increase the performance of your hard disk by up to 10%.

1 BEGINNING THE OPERATION

● Click on the **Start** button and select: **Programs, Accessories, System Tools,** and finally **Disk Defragmenter**.

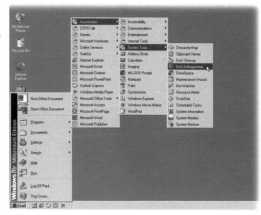

2 SELECTING THE DRIVE

● Disk Defragmenter asks which drive to defragment. You may choose to do more than one, but **Drive C** is selected here, which is the same drive that Disk Cleanup refers to as **HD1 (C:)**.

● Click on **OK**.

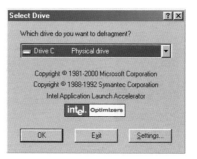

The Screen Saver

It is advisable to turn off your screen saver while running Disk Defragmenter . Every time the screen saver turns itself on, Disk Defragmenter is forced to start the defragmentation process again.

31 **Turning Off Your Screen Saver**

3 STARTING DEFRAGMENTING

● The defragmentation process starts. Microsoft Windows provides an animated graphic to accompany the process, which takes some time.

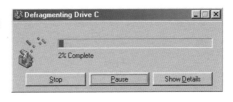

The Show Details button ●

4 CLICKING ON SHOW DETAILS

● Clicking on the Show Details button will give you a diagrammatic representation of the processes that are taking place. It may take a while for something to happen here.

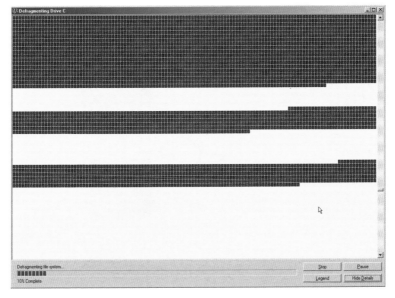

● To see an explanation of
what the graphics mean,
click on the **Legend** button.

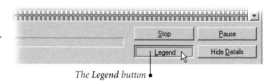

The Legend button ●

5 THE DEFRAG LEGEND PANEL

● The **Defrag Legend** panel
shows what the different
colored rectangles represent
in the main window.

● They are divided into the
locations where the files
belong; the files that are
being read, written, or have
been optimized; and free
and damaged areas of the
hard drive.

● You may close this panel
at any time without
interrupting the defrag-
mentation process.

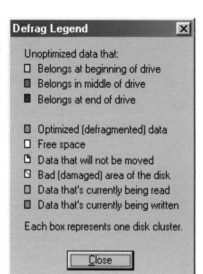

*The **Defrag Legend** panel shows, by using colored
blocks, a listing of the different file types, what is
happening to them, and explains where they belong.*

6 PAUSING THE PROCESS

● If you need to monitor
the process, but have to
leave your computer, you
can pause Disk Defrag-
menter at any time.

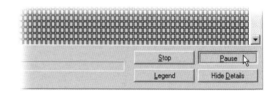

● Having clicked on **Pause**, the **Pause** button becomes a **Resume** button, which you can click when you are ready to proceed.

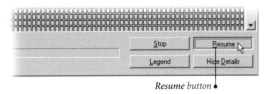

Resume button ●

7 SELECTING OTHER SETTINGS

● When you first start Disk Defragmenter, you can click on the **Settings** button for further options.

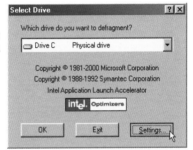

● The default settings in the **Disk Defragmenter Settings** dialog box are optimized for best results, and it is easiest to leave these settings unchanged.
● Click on **OK** when you are ready.

TURNING OFF YOUR SCREEN SAVER

First, right-click on the Desktop. In the pop-up menu, click on **Properties** at the foot of the menu. The **Display Properties** dialog box opens. Click on the **Screen Saver** tab at the top of the box. In the center of the box is a drop-down menu below the words **Screen Saver**. Click on the down-arrow to the right, scroll through the list until (**None**) is highlighted, and click on it. Click on **Apply** and then on **OK**. To reset the screen saver, select one from the **Screen Saver** drop-down menu, click on **Apply** and then on **OK**.

COMMERCIAL CLEANUP SOFTWARE

There are a number of utilities available on the market that can help keep your hard drive in good working order. Three of the best-known commercially available examples are Norton CleanSweep, McAfee Office, and MessCleaner.

NORTON CLEANSWEEP

Part of Symantec's Norton SystemWorks, this is one of the best pieces of software available for cleaning your hard drive. Although the program may cost a little more than some others, it is part of a suite of extremely useful diagnostic and repair tools. SystemWorks contains just about everything you could possibly need to keep your PC running at the peak of its performance. If you want peace of mind, you may consider Norton to be a worthwhile, long-term investment.

Further Reading
For further information on the various utilities in the Norton SystemWorks suite, by Symantec, please refer to *Maintaining Your PC* in this *DK Essential Computers* series.

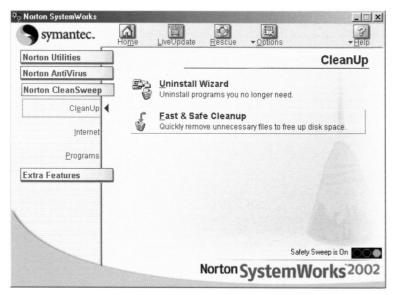

Norton SystemWorks includes, in Norton Utilities, an **Optimize Performance** section that allows you to run **Speed Disk** to help speed up your PC's performance. In the **Find and Fix Problems** section there are programs like **Norton System Doctor** and **Disk Doctor** to help you diagnose and repair common computer problems. Finally, in the **System Maintenance** section you'll find the **System Information program** which gathers useful data about your PC as well as **Wipe Info**, a program that permanently erases unwanted files from your PC.

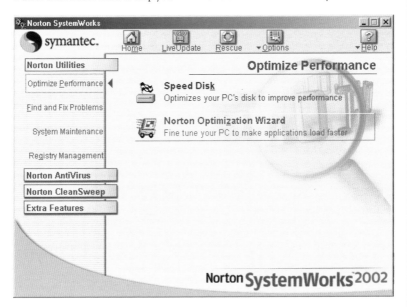

SOME OF THE NORTON CLEANSWEEP 2002 FEATURES

PROGRAMS
● The Backup Wizard creates a compressed back-up of a program..
● The Restore Wizard restores those files and items that Cleansweep has backed up.

INTERNET
● Removes disk-clogging Internet build-up including unwanted cookies, plug-ins and Active X controls.
● Uninstalls programs downloaded from the Internet.

CLEANUP:
● Quickly removes the majority of unnecessary files to free up useful disk space.
● The Uninstall Wizard removes programs that you no longer need.

MCAFEE UTILITIES

An appealing element of the McAfee suite of products is that it is all available via the world wide web, meaning that you do not have to make a physical purchase. By registering with McAfee at their website, it is very easy to download the utilities you choose. To register, you simply enter your email address, then later you will have to pay a yearly subscription. (The McAfee website has, at times, offered a free 14-day trial allowing you to try out the software.)

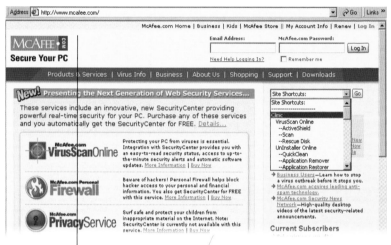

• *The* **Clinic** *tab*

At the McAfee homepage, click on the drop down menu on the right and choose **Clinic** from the list. You'll be presented with all the options available for maintaining your PC. Once you have made your choice, a **Security Warning** dialog box asks you to confirm that you want to install and run the selected software. The software will be down-loaded to the specified folder on your hard drive.

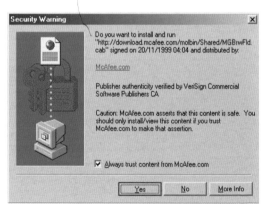

MESSCLEANER V2.03

MessCleaner V2.03 is freeware and is available for full download from http://www.fortunecity.com/skyscraper/jobbs/79/

As with its more expensive counterparts, MessCleaner has many utilities under its belt. The options include:

● Global option to delete files by sending them to the Recycle Bin.

● Option to display total and free space on your system drives when you place the mouse over your Messcleaner icon.

● Option to start Messcleaner on Windows startup.

● Option to select different colors and display times for screentips. Screentips are the small messages that appear when you position the mouse cursor over, for example, a toolbar button.

● Option to control how and what to delete when cleaning selected directories.

● Option to clean folders on startup and/or at predefined time periods according to a set schedule.

Try before you buy

It may be worth trying several different cleanup utilities before settling on one. By doing a search on the internet for PC maintenance, you should come up with other utilities, some of which are free.

MessCleaner V2.03
The MessCleaner dialog boxes are easy to read and fairly simple to understand.

Ready..

SCHEDULING TASKS

Now we can set all three of Window's cleaning utilities to run together with a Wizard. Although it looks complex and contains a lot of information, the Wizard is easy to use.

MAINTENANCE WIZARD

So far we have shown three Windows utilities: ScanDisk, Disk Cleanup, and Disk Defragmenter. As well as using them manually, they can also be set to run automatically. However, if they are set to run at night, the PC must be switched on.

The software icons from left to right: Disk Cleanup, Disk Defragmenter, Maintenance Wizard, and ScanDisk.

1 BEGINNING THE OPERATION

● To start using the **Maintenance Wizard**, click on the **Start** button, and then select: **Programs, Accessories, System Tools**, and finally **Maintenance Wizard**.

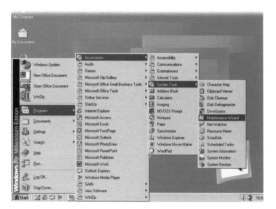

2 CHOOSING THE SETTING

● If you have previously set up a maintenance schedule, a window opens asking if you want either to perform maintenance now or to change the settings – which is the default option. Simply click on **OK**.

● A dialog box opens that explains what is about to happen and asks which setting you want to use: **Express**, which is the standard setting, or **Custom**, which allows you to select the operations you want to run and when you would like to run them.

● The Custom settings are dealt with later ⌐. Here, the **Express** settings are explained.

● With this option selected, click on **Next**.

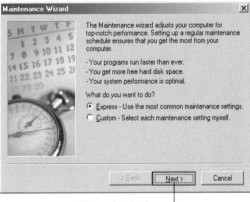

*Click on the **Next** button ●*

3 CHOOSING THE SCHEDULE

● The next dialog box asks when you wish to run the **Maintenance Wizard**. For this example, **Evenings – 8.00 PM to 11.00 PM** is selected.

● Remember, this means that you must have your machine switched on at this time.

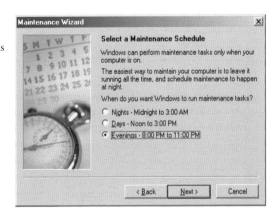

● Click on the **Next** button once you are satisfied with your selection.

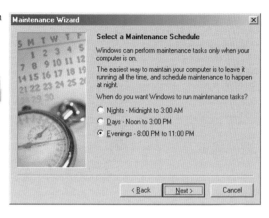

Select a Maintenance Schedule

Windows can perform maintenance tasks only when your computer is on.

The easiest way to maintain your computer is to leave it running all the time, and schedule maintenance to happen at night.

When do you want Windows to run maintenance tasks?

○ Nights - Midnight to 3:00 AM
○ Days - Noon to 3:00 PM
◉ Evenings - 8:00 PM to 11:00 PM

< Back   Next >   Cancel

4 THE TASKS AND THE UTILITIES

● **Maintenance Wizard** tells you the tasks that it will carry out. The utilities it uses are Disk Defragmenter, to speed up your most frequently used programs, ScanDisk, to check your hard disk for errors, and Disk Cleanup, to delete any unnecessary files.

In the background
Disk Defragmenter will run in the background while you continue to work on files, though your computer will operate more slowly. However, if you save or delete files, or change the contents of the hard disk in any way, Disk Defragmenter will start its procedure over again

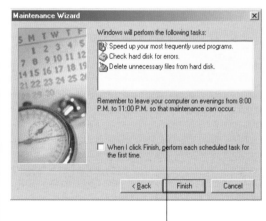

Windows will perform the following tasks:

🖩 Speed up your most frequently used programs.
🖫 Check hard disk for errors.
🖫 Delete unnecessary files from hard disk.

Remember to leave your computer on evenings from 8:00 P.M. to 11:00 P.M. so that maintenance can occur.

☐ When I click Finish, perform each scheduled task for the first time.

< Back   Finish   Cancel

*Note that **Maintenance Wizard** confirms the time that you have set it to run*

5 RUN THE WIZARD NOW?

● If you want to run the Wizard immediately after finishing the setting up procedure, click in that check box. Otherwise, leave it empty.

● When you have made your choices, click on the **Finish** button.

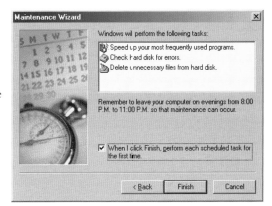

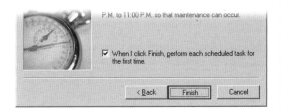

6 THE WIZARD SETS TO WORK

● If you chose to run the Wizard now, it briefly displays a panel confirming its actions.

● The Maintenance Wizard then starts its cleanup operations.

● The first utility to be used is Disk Cleanup.

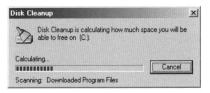

● Second, ScanDisk begins its examination of the hard drive, in this case, **Hd1** (**C:**). As this is an automatic procedure, there's no need to click on any buttons; but there is a **Cancel** button available if you need to terminate the operation.

● Finally, Disk Defragmenter runs while displaying its animated graphics.

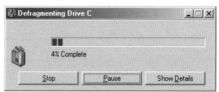

USING THE CUSTOM SETTINGS

Once you have become accustomed to using the **Express** settings, it's possible to move on to using the **Custom** settings

where you can have more control over how the software supplied with Windows operates on your PC.

SETTING UP SCHEDULES

The custom settings panel of the Maintenance Wizard gives more options, such as setting up schedules for Disk Defragmenter, ScanDisk, and Disk Cleanup.

1 BEGINNING THE OPERATION

● Click on the **Start** button, then select: **Programs, Accessories, System Tools**, and finally **Maintenance Wizard**.

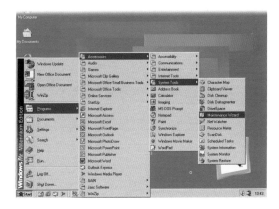

2 SELECTING THE CUSTOM OPTION

● The **Maintenance Wizard** dialog box opens.
● Click on the **Custom** radio button.

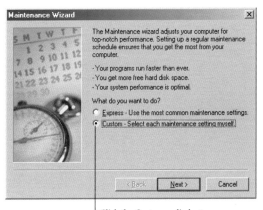

●*Click the **Custom** radio button*

● Click on the **Next** button to move on to setting up your personal preferences.

3 START WINDOWS MORE QUICKLY

● One aspect of the customizing option in the **Maintenance Wizard** is that you are offered the opportunity to make Windows start more quickly.

● Use the scroll bar to display the applications that you want to prevent from opening. Any application without a check mark will not open when you boot your PC.

● Click on the **Next** button when you have made your selections.

Use the scroll bar to select the options that you require

4 DEFRAGMENTER SCHEDULE

● This screen allows you to set a schedule for running Disk Defragmenter.

● If you want to run the Disk Defragmenter from within the **Maintenance Wizard**, then click in the **Yes, defragment my disk regularly** radio button.

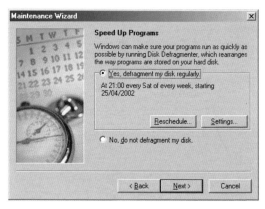

5 CHOOSING TO RESCHEDULE

● You may wish to change the **Maintenance Wizard's** default schedule setting. If so, click on the **Reschedule** button.

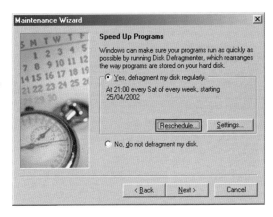

6 CHANGING THE SCHEDULE

● The **Reschedule** dialog box opens. The **Maintenance Wizard** provides default settings for Disk Defragmenter to run, which include running the software once a week and starting at 1 AM each Saturday. However, there are many options that you can customize.

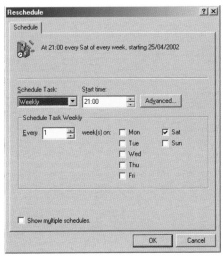

● With normal use, you only need to run Disk Defragmenter monthly. Click on the down arrow of the **Schedule Task** box, and select **Monthly**.

● When you have finished, click **OK** to take you back to the main **Wizard** screen.

● The **Maintenance Wizard** window confirms your settings, so simply click on **Next**.

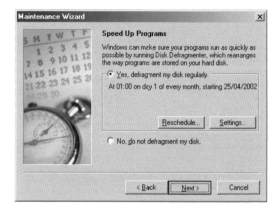

7 SCHEDULING SCANDISK

● Now we can set a schedule for ScanDisk, using the procedure shown in the previous step.

● Click on **Reschedule** if you want to reset this, otherwise click on **Next**.

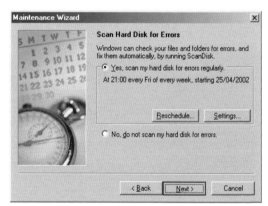

8 SCHEDULING DISK CLEANUP

● Again, you can either reschedule Disk Cleanup or click on **Next** if you are happy with the settings.

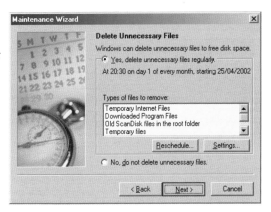

● By putting a checkmark in the check box **When I click Finish, perform each scheduled task for the first time**, Maintenance Wizard will run through its entire routine.

● If you are happy simply to let **Maintenance Wizard** run at the times that you have designated, then leave the check box blank and click on **Finish**.

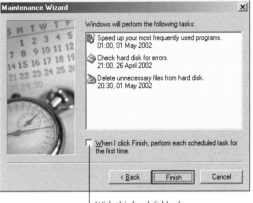

● With this box left blank,
Maintenance Wizard will not run
when you click on Finish

MAKING BACKUPS

Computers fail for many reasons, and when they do
it's important that you have a copy of your work, applications,
and, more importantly, your operating system.

WHAT DOES BACKING UP MEAN?

Making a backup, in its simplest form, involves copying all the information held on your computer from your hard drive to removable, portable media, such as a disk or magnetic tape, that can be removed from the computer and stored.

BACKUP MEDIA

The best way to recover from a major accident is to have a comprehensive backup on disk or tape. If the computer is stolen or irretrievably damaged, you should be able to rebuild your data from the backup disks. The main types of removable media suitable for backing up a home PC are: Zip, DAT tapes, CD-R (Compact Disk Recordable), and DVD. Although DAT and DVD are suitable backup devices for the office, they may be larger than necessary for the home user. A CD writer is relatively cheap, and blank CDs in bulk cost less than blank audio tapes. Zip drives are also relatively inexpensive. Floppy disks are less suitable for backing up because of their limited capacity. A Zip disk can hold almost 100 times the data of a floppy disk, and a CD can hold up to 740 times as much.

When choosing a backup medium, you should take into account the cost of the drive and the disks, and the storage capacity that each type offers.

MICROSOFT BACKUP

Microsoft Backup is part of Windows Me and easily allows you to make a backup of your work onto many different types of media including Zip disks and removable

hard drives. It also allows you to compress the files as they are copied. The compression process means that files take up less space on your storage tape or drive.

1 FINDING BACKUP

● Microsoft Backup can be found by clicking on the **Start** button, then selecting **Programs, Accessories, System Tools,** and then **Backup.**

● Insert a blank disk into your floppy disk drive.

INSTALLING MICROSOFT BACKUP FROM THE WINDOWS ME CD

To install Microsoft Backup from the Windows Me CD, insert the CD into the drive and click the **Add/Remove Software** button when the options appear. In the next window, choose the **Windows Setup** tab. In this window, scroll down to find **System**

Tools. Double-click on **System Tools** to open that window. **Backup** will probably be at the top of a list in that window. Ensure that this box is checked and click on **OK.** In the next window, click on **Apply** and Microsoft Backup will be installed on your computer.

FLOPPY DISKS

On the next few pages, we will be using a floppy disk to back up a file, mainly because almost everyone will have a floppy drive. However, as has already been mentioned, we do not recommend using a floppy disk to make backups of files as their capacity is very limited.

2 THE MAIN SCREEN

● Two windows appear: the main backup screen explains what a backup is, and asks what you would like to do. Here, we want to create a new backup, so click on that radio button and then on **OK**.

Click on this radio button to create a new backup

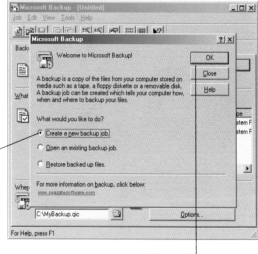

Click on OK

3 THE BACKUP WIZARD

● The next screen to appear is the **Backup Wizard**. If you have a large capacity backup medium, such as a CD writer, then you can back up the entire contents of your computer by using the first option. In this example, a single file is to be backed up onto a floppy disk.

● Select the second option of selecting the files to be backed up by clicking on its radio button, then click on **Next**.

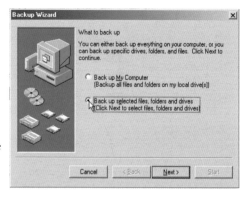

4 LOCATING THE FILES

● As only selected items have been chosen to be backed up, they need to be found on the computer. Beneath **What to back up**, click on the plus signs to open folders. In this case, the C: drive has been selected, followed by the **My Documents** folder, and then the **My Pictures** folder.

● Double-click the folder, and the image file **Flowers** is listed on the right. As this is the file to be backed up, place a checkmark in the box next to it. Then click on **Start**.

Click on the plus signs to open each folder; once the folder is open the plus signs become minus signs

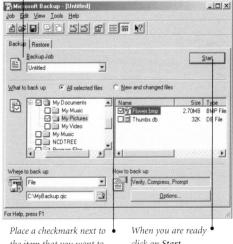

Place a checkmark next to the item that you want to back up

*When you are ready click on **Start***

5 SELECTED FILES

● For the next step, choose to back up **All selected files** and click on **Next**.

*Choose **All selected files***

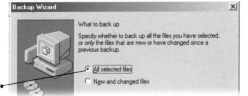

6 WHERE TO BACK UP?

● We need to tell the Wizard where to back up the files. If the floppy drive is already shown, click on **Next**. If it is not, click on the **Folder** button to bring up the **Where to back up** dialog box.

The Folder button

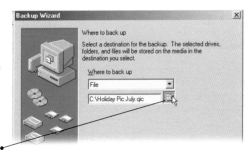

7 SELECTING THE DRIVE

● The **Where to back up** dialog box opens.
● Select your floppy drive (usually the A: drive) using the pull-down menu.

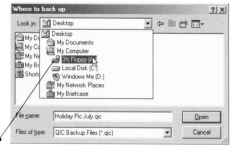

The floppy drive

● Click on the **Open** button.

8 NAMING THE FILE

● You are returned to the **Backup Wizard** window.
● Click on the **Next** button.

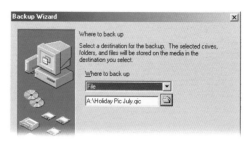

9 CHECKING AND CORRECTING

● Select both of the options in this dialog box. The first one checks to make sure that the file has been copied over correctly, the second option compresses the file.
● Click on the **Next** button.

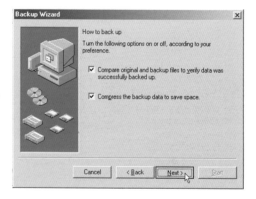

10 CHOOSING A NAME

● Using the drop-down menu, select a name for the backup, in this instance we have chosen to use the date. You can type your own choice of name.
● Click on the **Start** button.

Drop-down menu ●

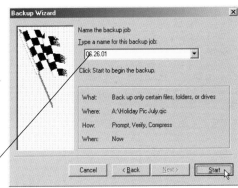

11 THE PROGRESS WINDOW

● The **Backup Wizard** now presents you with a dialog box that shows the progress of the backup operation. As we only have one file to back up, the whole process is completed very quickly.

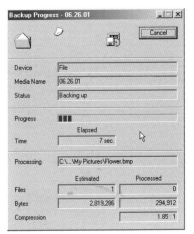

12 FINISHING THE TASK

● An alert panel appears confirming that the backup is finished. Click on **OK** once more to exit the program, then close the main backup window.

VIRUSES

We are all susceptible to computer viruses that can come to us as a result of downloading software from the internet, or passing from computer to computer by disk or email.

THE RISKS OF A VIRUS

A computer virus is a program or piece of code that can attach itself to programs on your computer. Some viruses can be considered almost harmless, perhaps throwing up joke messages; but some can delete a few or all of the files on the hard drive, causing a complete system failure known as a crash. A system failure may render your PC completely inoperable – unable even to boot up.

HOW DOES A VIRUS OCCUR?

A computer virus will have been written by someone. Most viruses start as small programs that lie hidden, attached to an application on your computer, until they are activated by running the application. The virus looks for another program to infect. It then changes each program so that it, too, contains a copy of the virus and waits for the next unsuspecting victim. Viruses are created in different ways, that is, they can infect and affect different parts of your computer. For example, a program virus will infect program files. A program file will have a file ending (or extension) such as .COM (command file) or .EXE (executable file). An executable file is the kind of file that you would use to open an application by double-clicking on it. Program viruses are common because they are easier to write.

HOW DOES A VIRUS GET ONTO MY MACHINE?

There are many potential sources that may contain a virus. A borrowed piece of software or a zip or floppy disk may contain a virus. Other ways in which a virus can infect a computer include downloading files from the internet, from a private bulletin board, or by opening an infected email.Viruses used to be conveyed from computer to computer only by executable program files. However, newer viruses, known as "macro" viruses, can exist in any document created by applications, such as Microsoft Word, which use a macro language.

1 The virus is designed and created by a programmer, who will probably start the trail of destruction by means of mass emailing. The emails may have file attachments that contain the virus.

2 The emails are received and the attachments are opened by the recipients. The virus contaminates the person's computer.

4 Once again, the mail is opened and the virus attaches itself to the new computer. The unsuspecting culprit may email his friends or give copies of the file and the virus now begins to take effect.

3 The file attachment may be passed to a friend via floppy disk or again by email. The virus then spreads.

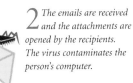

The virus is not selective. Once it has been passed to your system via a floppy disk, downloaded on a piece of software from the internet, or from an email, it will be only a matter of time before it triggers itself and begins to infect your computer.

WHAT DOES A VIRUS CONTAIN?

Replication engine: A successful virus makes copies of itself that move on to other computers.

Protection: A virus protects itself from detection by amending sectors on the hard drive to conceal its presence.

Trigger: The event that activates the virus may be a date and time that is read by the virus from the system clock, or by an action being repeated a certain number of times by the user.

Payload: This is the damage that the virus has been set to cause, which may or may not include loss of data.

VIRUS DEFINITIONS

Boot sector viruses: These are spread when there is an infected floppy disk, bootable or not, in the disk drive when a computer is booted. The virus is copied to the hard drive where it moves the original boot sector to another part of the disk and takes over the computer's operations.

Program viruses: These attach themselves to program files. Running them loads the virus into memory where it replicates.

Macro viruses: These viruses infect files created by applications that use a macro language, such as Microsoft Word. The virus issues commands that are accepted, understood, and executed as valid macros by the application.

Multipartite viruses: These combine the features of boot sector viruses and program viruses. They are able to move in either direction between the boot sector and applications on the hard drive.

SOME KNOWN VIRUSES

AMBULANCE

Ambulance has also been known as RedX and Red Cross. It infects command files (these are invisible files that make your computer work). It is a rare virus that displays a moving ambulance and plays a siren sound.

AVALON

Again, Avalon infects command files, but it also infects executable files. This virus has a trigger that is set to work on the 31st of any month. It can render the drive useless and nonbootable.

ZELU

Zelu infects all files but is also a rare virus. It is known as a Trojan horse and is not strictly a virus, although it has the same effect. The file is normally called Y2K.EXE and pretends to be a year 2000 compatibility checker. After software containing the virus has been installed and is run, the virus flashes file names across the bottom of the screen pretending to check them, but in reality it is overwriting and destroying them. You are then informed that you have been fooled and hit with a virus. As we are in the third millennium, this virus is no longer a real threat.

PARITY BOOT

This virus is fairly common. Once on your system, it checks every hour to see if it has infected a floppy disk. If it hasn't, then it displays a message on your screen that says "Parity Check," and causes your computer to crash.

VBS/NEWLOVE.A

This virus lodges itself in the Windows folder when it is first run following infection of your hard drive. It adopts a file name from the Recent Documents folder, or creates a random file name. The virus sends copies of itself to all entries in the address book by using Outlook Express. All drives connected to the computer are searched, and files are replaced by copies of the virus; the extension .VBS is added to the file name.

ANTIVIRUS SOFTWARE

There are a number of antivirus applications available, and some are available free over the internet. However, these tend to detect only the more common viruses. If you require software that is more comprehensive and able to detect the rarer viruses, it is advisable to use an industry-standard virus detector.

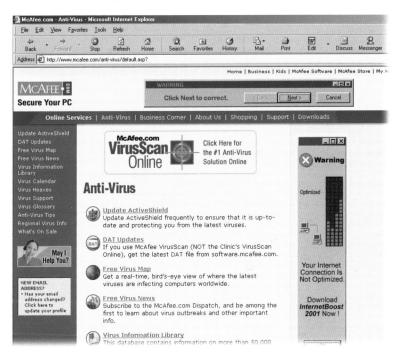

MORE FROM MCAFEE

McAfee's website, **www.mcafee.com**, invites you to download and upgrade antivirus software, much of which is offered on a two-week, free trial period. The site also provides opportunities to report viruses, to browse through their database of 50,000 known viruses, and to view a virus glossary of terms and virus definitions. The virus calendar gives the trigger dates of virus payloads. Also available is a database of hoax viruses.

NORTON ANTIVIRUS

Norton AntiVirus is one of the most popular and well-known antivirus software packages available. Norton offers virtually unrivaled protection, a very user-friendly interface, and simple updating that is available over the internet.

EASILY UPDATABLE

Norton AntiVirus is a utility available within the Norton SystemWorks suite. It gives protection while you are surfing the internet or retrieving information from floppy disks. It can even be set up to scan incoming emails and their attachments.

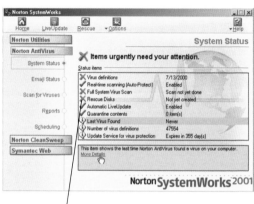

System Status •
System Status determines exactly what measures you should take to protect your PC.

• Once you have clicked on the **More Details** link, the **System Status Details** dialog box opens and tells you how long ago it was since a virus was found on your computer. Click on **OK** to close the window.

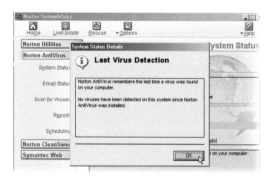

● Click on an item in the list (in this instance we have clicked on **Virus Definitions**), and then on **More Items**, which appears at the bottom of the panel.

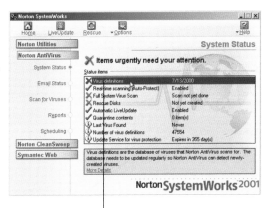

Select the items that you wish to update.

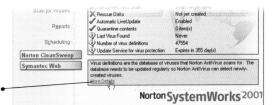

Click on the More Details text link.

● You are once again presented with the **Systems Status Details** window. This time however, you are offered the chance to update your virus definitions, these will be downloaded from the internet and will protect you against the newest viruses. Click the **Yes** button to start the process.

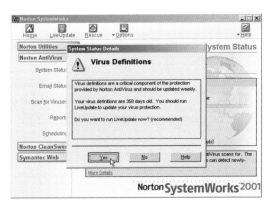

ABOUT STARTUP DISKS

**One of the most important accessories for your computer
setup, and probably the one that is most overlooked as far
as looking after your PC is concerned, is a startup disk.**

WITH SAFETY IN MIND

There is a small chance that one day your hard drive will fail, for one of several possible reasons, and your PC will be unable to start on its own. It is therefore very important that you create a startup disk that can be used to boot your computer because with a failed hard drive, a startup disk will be your only resource. By following a few easy instructions, you can avoid considerable problems, loss of time, and possible loss of data. Once created, do not forget where the disk is.

WHAT IS A STARTUP DISK?

A computer may fail to start if the system files become corrupted. There can be many reasons for this happening. For example, you may be unlucky enough to have your hard drive infected by a virus, or you may have installed some new software incorrectly, causing a software conflict.

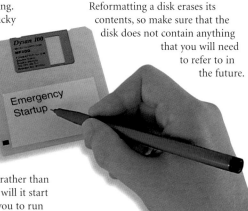

A startup disk is created on a standard 3½-inch floppy disk. With a startup disk, your computer will boot from that rather than from the hard drive. Not only will it start your computer, it also allows you to run some diagnostic programs to fix problems if necessary. It is best to use a new disk for this task, but if you are going to use an old disk, it first needs to be reformatted. Reformatting a disk erases its contents, so make sure that the disk does not contain anything that you will need to refer to in the future.

FORMATTING A FLOPPY DISK

Although you can easily erase items from a floppy disk, it can become fragmented over time and can contain all kinds of hidden litter, which could even corrupt the disk. It is therefore a good move, especially when creating something as important as a startup disk, to reformat an old disk.

1 INSERTING THE FLOPPY DISK

● Take a floppy disk and insert it into the floppy disk drive.

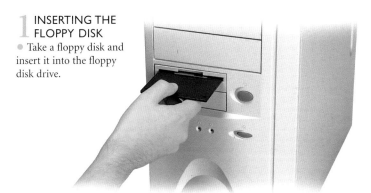

2 OPENING MY COMPUTER

● Double-click on the **My Computer** icon on the Desktop.

3 THE FLOPPY DISK ICON

● The **My Computer** window opens. If you need to copy any files from the floppy disk, do so now. If you don't need anything from the disk, click on the 3½ **Floppy (A:)** icon.

4 SELECTING FORMAT

● Click on **File** in the menu bar and select **Format** from the drop-down menu.

5 SELECTING THE TYPE OF FORMAT

● The **Format - 3½ Floppy (A:)** dialog box opens. Click on the **Full** radio button for a full format.

Click on Full

● Click on the **Start** button to begin the process.

Click on Start

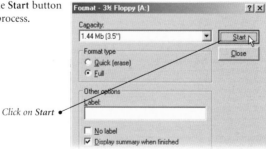

6 INITIALIZE AND FORMAT

● Windows goes through an initialization process and then begins to format the disk. A bar shows how far the formatting has progressed.

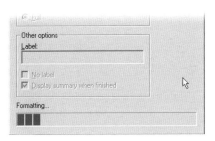

7 FORMAT RESULTS

● At the end of the process, the **Format Results** box is displayed. This shows how much free space is available on the newly formatted disk. Click on **Close**, then close any other windows. Eject the floppy disk from the drive and keep it in a safe place.

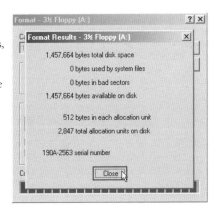

KEEPING THOSE DISKS SAFE

The best thing to do with a new startup disk is to label it clearly and store it with the original system disks, CDs, printer drivers, and Windows software. In this way, you will always know where to find the disk in an emergency.

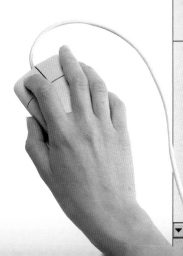

MAKING A STARTUP DISK

Now we have a newly formatted disk, it can be made into a startup disk. This process will probably take a maximum of 10 minutes to complete, and should only require one floppy disk. You may need your Windows Me CD available.

1 FIRST STEPS

● To begin the process of making a startup disk, click on the **Start** button, select **Settings** from the pop-up menu, then **Control Panel.**
● From the **Control Menu,** double click on **Add/Remove Programs**

2 THE ADD/REMOVE PROGRAMS PANEL

● The **Add/Remove Programs Properties** dialog box opens. Click on the **Startup Disk** tab.

3 CREATING THE STARTUP DISK

● The **Startup Disk** tab gives you brief details about a startup disk. Click on the **Create Disk** button.

● Windows may ask you to insert the Windows Me CD. Click on **OK** when you've done so.

● Windows begins to prepare the necessary startup files to copy onto the disk.

*Click on **Create Disk***

4 INSERTING THE DISK

● When Windows is ready, the **Insert Disk** dialog box appears asking you to insert a disk. Click on **OK** when you have inserted the newly formatted floppy disk into the drive.

5 COPYING FILES AND DATA

● Windows continues the process by loading all the necessary files and data onto the floppy disk.

● When the process has been completed, click on **OK** and take the floppy disk out of the drive.

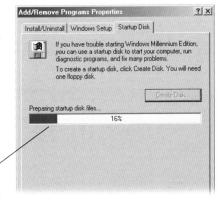

Windows runs through its procedure and continues preparing the startup disk files

EMERGENCY MEASURES

In this chapter, we will discuss some emergency measures that can be applied, using your startup disk, in the event that your computer does not operate properly or will not start at all.

USING SYSTEM RESTORE

System Restore is new to Windows Me and gives you the opportunity to return your PC to a state in which it was working in a satisfactory manner, therefore undoing things that may have caused problems. For instance, you may have installed a new piece of software that has damaged the way your monitor driver operates, corrupting it in some way. System Restore will try to return your computer to a stage before the install.

You can create your own restore points or you can use those already on your PC. The latter are known as System Checkpoints, and they are created when new software is installed.

1 USING SYSTEM CHECKPOINTS

● First, go to the **Start** menu, and then choose **Programs, Accessories, System Tools**, and, finally, **System Restore**.

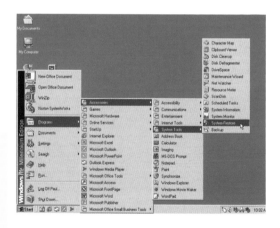

Revoke the restore...
If you perform a restore and are not happy with the results, you can always revert back to the stage from which you performed the restore!

2 CHOOSING A RESTORE POINT

● You have two choices here. The first is to restore your PC to a time that has been determined by your computer or you can create your own restore point.

● If you have a problem with your PC at the moment, select the **Restore my computer to an earlier time** button and then click on **Next**.

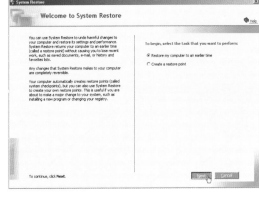

3 CHOOSING A DATE

● A calendar appears. In this example, no restore points have been created by the user – only System Checkpoints are available. These are shown as slightly bolder numbers in the calendar.

● To restore your PC to one of theses dates, click on the number and then the **Next** button.

● Before you continue, you will be asked to make sure that you do not have any applications open at this time. When you are ready, click on the **Next** button.

● Your computer begins the restore routine, which may take a while. Your computer will then automatically restart.

CREATING YOUR OWN RESTORE POINT

You can create a restore point on your PC at any time. However, the best time is probably when you are happy that everything is operating smoothly, or perhaps before you are about to perform a large install of some new software, something that may damage the smooth running of your computer.

1 FROM THE BEGINNING
● First, go to the **Start** menu, and then choose **Programs, Accessories, Systems Tools**, and, finally, **System Restore**.

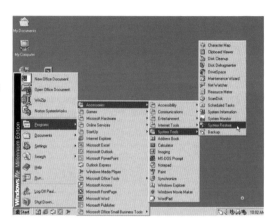

2 CREATING A RESTORE POINT
● In the main window select the **Create a restore point** button and then click on the **Next** button.

3 NAMING THE RESTORE POINT

● The next window opens and a cursor flashes in a text panel. Give your restore point a name, for example, **My first restore point**.

● When you have finished, click on the **Next** button.

● The restore point is created and you are asked to confirm your restore point name. If you are not happy with it, then click the **Back** button and rename it.

● If you are happy with the name, click on the **OK** button.

MICROSOFT UPDATE

It is worth using the Microsoft Update feature on your PC, as frequent software updates are available for items such as System Restore. Bugs are fixed and new functionality added to make the software smoother and easier to use.

BOOT FROM THE STARTUP DISK

Using the restore function shown on the previous pages is all very well if the problem that you encountered can be solved in that manner, however, if your hard drive fails, the consequences can range from an emergency boot to disk replacement. As you have made a startup disk, you may be able to at least start the computer and restore some data even if you haven't made a backup.

1 READY TO BEGIN?

● First, turn your computer off completely using the power switch on the front.

NO GUARANTEES

There is never any fail-safe way of making your machine crash-proof. You may find, for example, that even when you do manage to boot from the startup disk, your machine is not working well. This could be a hardware problem and you should consult your local supplier. On the other hand, you may be fortunate and only need to run a repair utility to restore your hard drive.

2 INSERTING THE STARTUP DISK

● Put your startup floppy disk into the disk drive and then turn your machine on.

3 INSERT THE WINDOWS CD

● Once your machine is starting up, open the CD drawer and insert your Windows Me CD.

4 NOW WHAT HAPPENS?

● You may be alarmed at the images that your PC now displays onscreen as you watch, but there's no need to worry, as this is standard practice. Your PC is only going through a routine of checking that it has all the files that it needs.

● Your PC boots up in what is known as MS-DOS mode (using the startup floppy disk), which is the long-established operating system that is still used as the backbone of Windows.

● In the Windows Me Startup Menu, you are offered four options:
1. Help
2. Start computer with CD-ROM support.
3. Start computer without CD-ROM support.
4. Minimal boot.

At this prompt, the Startup Menu allows you to start your system, possibly with CD-ROM support.

```
Microsoft Windows Me Startup Menu
==============================
1. Help
2. Start computer with CD-ROM support
3. Start computer without CD-ROM support
4. Minimal boot
Enter a choice: 1          Time remaining: 24
```

● Using the cursor keys, select option number 2; **Start computer with CD-ROM support** and then press the enter key.

5 UP AND RUNNING

● Your computer will now start with CD-ROM support, and the startup disk will find the appropriate software for your CD-ROM drive.

ON-SCREEEN PROMPTS

On screen prompts take you through the tasks that will try to correct the problems that caused your PC to die. There are no guarantees that the problem won't occur again. You may have irreparable damage to your hard disk, in which case, you should consult a qualified technician.

GLOSSARY

APPLICATION
Another term for a piece of software.

ATTACHMENT
Almost any type of file can be sent within an email by "attaching" it to a message that you send.

COMPRESSION
A system of reducing the size of a computer file, often to make an image faster to download.

CRASH
The term applied when a computer suddenly stops working during a routine operation. Typical signs of a crash include a "freeze" or "lockup," in which the PC appears to be running but will not allow any movement of the pointer or use of the keyboard.

DEFRAGMENTING
The process of reassembling and arranging badly distributed files on a hard drive.

DISK CLEANUP
A utility within the Windows Me system tools, used for deleting unnecessary files and cleaning up a hard drive.

DISK DEFRAGMENTER
Part of the Windows Me operating system. Disk Defragmenter is used to re-assemble badly distributed files on a hard drive.

DOWNLOAD
The transfer of data from one computer to another. Your browser downloads HTML code and graphics to display a page.

EMAIL (ELECTRONIC MAIL)
The system of sending electronic messages between computers via the internet.

GIF (GRAPHICS INTERCHANGE FORMAT)
A widely used file format for web-based images.

HARD DRIVE
Sometimes known as the hard disk, a large capacity primary drive used to store data.

HARDWARE
Hardware is the part of a computer that you can physically see or touch.

INSTALLING
The process of "loading" an item of software onto a hard drive. See uninstalling.

INTERNET
The network of interconnected computers that communicate using the TCP/IP protocol.

JPEG (JOINT PHOTO-GRAPHIC EXPERTS GROUP)
A file format for web-based images, particularly for photographic images.

PATH
The address of a file on a computer system.

PERIPHERAL
A piece of equipment used for either input (a keyboard or scanner)or output (a printer or monitor), which can be connected to your computer.

RADIO BUTTON
Small onscreen button within an application that visibly turns on and off when clicked with a mouse.

SCANDISK
Part of the Windows Me operating system, ScanDisk checks for and corrects damaged files.

SOFTWARE
A computer needs software for it to function. Software comes in many forms - from simple utilities to immense computer games.

SYSTEM
A computer system as a whole, consisting of all the major components that make up the PC workstation.

SYSTEM TOOLS
The items contained within Windows Me, and accessed from the Start menu, that insure the safe running and maintenance of the computer system.

UNINSTALLING
The process of removing an item of software from the hard drive by deleting all its files.

VIRUS
A program or piece of computer code deliberately created and distributed to destroy or disorganize data on other computer systems.

WEBSITE
A collection of web pages that are linked together, and possibly to other websites, by hyperlinks.

WIZARD
A series of prompts to accomplish a specific task.

INDEX

ACKNOWLEDGMENTS

PUBLISHER'S ACKNOWLEDGMENTS
Dorling Kindersley would like to thank the following:
Paul Mattock of APM, Brighton, for commissioned photography.
Microsoft Corporation for permission to reproduce screens
from within Microsoft® Windows® Me.
Symantec Corporation for permission to reproduce screens
from within Norton SystemWorks 2000. McAfee.com; fortunecity.com

*Every effort has been made to trace the copyright holders.
The publisher apologizes for any unintentional omissions and would be pleased,
in such cases, to place an acknowledgment in future editions of this book.*